"Every thoughtful, biblical foll [...] Larry Dixon's loving corrective to F [...] atest dangers in interpreting the Bi [...] [...]ure to prove your point, in exclusion of other Scripture passages. This, I believe, is Rob Bell's greatest error when it comes to the subject of universalism. Larry Dixon, on the other hand, seeks to bring *all* of Scripture to bear on this important subject."

Dr. George Murray
Chancellor, Columbia International University

"As a psychiatrist, I have a keen interest in helping people feel better mentally and emotionally, but this 'feeling better' is only a cruel illusion if it is obtained by sacrificing truth. There are times that physicians must be the bearers of bad news. We do this so that patients can make well-informed, wise decisions about their health and future. Treating cancer with pain-killers can provide temporary relief, but it doesn't change the reality that cancer will kill unless one consents to aggressive and painful interventions. The same is true when dealing with the subject of Hell. Ignoring it will surely make you and me feel better -- for a time. There is, however, no escaping its ultimate reality. That is why I am so thankful for Dr. Larry Dixon's newest book, *Farewell, Rob Bell*. Concise yet packed with sound doctrine and logical arguments against universalism, this book will equip you with the truth necessary to secure lasting healing and redemption, not a temporary band-aid for the consequences of sin."

David Livingstone Henderson, M.D.
Co-author of *Finding Purpose Beyond Our Pain*
Chair of Psychology, Criswell College
Adjunct Professor, Dallas Theological Seminary

Larry Dixon's response to Rob Bell's pop-theological LOVE WINS is theologically informed, corrective, and considerate. Who ought to read his reply? Every Jesus follower attracted to Bell's point of view, and every believer who wants to be equipped to deal with those who are. Dixon has the theological training and experience to handle in one concise manuscript both the cogent biblical doctrines themselves and the characterization given them in Bell's book.

Dr. Barry Creamer, Professor of Humanities, Criswell College
Host of Radio Program "Coffee with Creamer"

Dr. Larry Dixon's unenviable task is the defense of an unpopular doctrine. After all, who wants to argue against a well-loved pastor for the eternal punishment of unregenerate man? But if a central tenet of God's truth is being misrepresented, Dixon has to speak up. Even so, his approach to Bell and this sensitive subject is careful, respectful, and (as always) thoroughly scriptural. Thank you, Larry, for not remaining silent.

Pastor Paul Cochrane
Woodland Hills Community Church
Columbia, SC

"Farewell, Rob Bell:" A Biblical Response to *Love Wins*

Larry Dixon, Ph.D.

THEOMEDIAN RESOURCES
WHERE GOD'S TRUTH JOYFULLY MAKES SENSE

Columbia, South Carolina

"Farewell, Rob Bell": A Biblical Response to *Love Wins*

THEOMEDIAN RESOURCES
117 Norse Way
Columbia, SC 29229
http://larrydixon.wordpress.com/

THEOMEDIAN RESOURCES is a combination of the terms "theologian" + "comedian." The study of God's truths ought to be enjoyable. Theology is not boring; theologians are boring. "It is, indeed, a shame to bore God's people with God's Word." (Daryl Busby).

Cover art by Ron Wheeler of CartoonWorks.com.

First printing: August 2011

ISBN-13: 978-1461191667

—

CONTENTS

—

FOREWORD

Several times a month Larry Dixon and I would go to Angelo's to get some broasted chicken and talk about online courses, theology and ideas for books. Invariably we would also end up discussing the newest twists in world affairs and the latest heretical trends to hit the news.

Recently, Larry reviewed some of his ideas with me for a chapel message he was preparing on Rob Bell's book, *Love Wins*. I had seen the video that Rob Bell had produced introducing his book and I had read some early reviews, but Larry helped me understand the urgency and the significance of a biblical critique of Bell's universalistic tendencies. I deal with cults and aberrant theological views, and it became evident through Larry's explanations that Bell's theological shortcomings have caused him to not only misunderstand Scripture but to twist it to the extent that his conclusions would lead Christians further away from the truth. Bell makes the fatal mistake of viewing heaven and hell from man's perspective rather than from God's eternal perspective.

It was so helpful for me to sit there at Angelo's and listen to Larry go point by point through the problems presented by Bell's teachings and then hear him give sound theological reasons as to why they were problematic and even heretical. The genius in Larry's teaching is that he is able to explore difficult theological themes and then explain them in practical ways, often with his trademark humor. This is true of this book, which is an expanded version of his chapel message on the dangers of Rob Bell's popular ideas. Every thinking Christian needs to understand what is really at stake in Bell's aberrant theology, and Larry Dixon's book is a great way to begin your exploration. But be sure to get some broasted chicken to go with the book. It will make it go down a little easier.

Daniel Janosik, Ph.D.
Associate Professor of Apologetics and Islamic Studies and
Director of Online Education at Southern Evangelical Seminary

DEDICATION

I gratefully dedicate this book to my friend and colleague Dr. Terry Hulbert of Columbia International University Seminary and School of Missions.

Even though I was never privileged to take a course from him, for the last several years we have enjoyed coffee and theological discussion together approximately three times a week.

He continually thanked me for providing coffee; he provided his life experience – and I got the better deal!

INTRODUCTION

"Farewell, Rob Bell":[1]
A Biblical Response to *Love Wins*

Please do not panic -- but you must remain in your seats! We are in control of this aircraft now and no one will get hurt if you do exactly as you are told. This plane is being hijacked!"

Imagine how you would react if you were a passenger on that airplane. How much worse would you feel if you realized you were one of the hijackers? A hijacker puts the lives of others in grave danger, attempting to take control of that which does not belong to him.

According to Rob Bell in *Love Wins: A Book about Heaven, Hell, and the Fate of Every Person Who Ever Lived* (HarperOne, 2011), if you are an Evangelical Christian, you are a theological hijacker of the Jesus story. And all Evangelicals are guilty of replacing that story with one that consigns the majority of the human race to hell. Bell believes that the very idea that billions will suffer eternally isn't a very good story, minimizes the greatness of God, and is, well, to use his word, *toxic*. So, Mr. or Mrs. Toxic Evangelical Hijacker, how do you feel?

The Goal of This Book:

The Evangelical world seems to be dividing very quickly into the pro-Bellums and the ante-Bellums, but that's not what this book is about. Reactions to *Love Wins* have run the gamut from "this is a much-needed and thoroughly biblical book" to "let's hang 'em and let's hang 'em high!" With apologies to Clint Eastwood, I haven't really heard of any who want to hang Bell, but there is good, bad, and ugly in this book resulting in some very strong reactions to its theology.

Eugene Peterson, author of *The Message*, provided a jacket blurb for *Love Wins* which says, "It isn't easy to develop a biblical imagination that takes in the comprehensive and eternal work of Christ. . . . Rob Bell goes a long way in helping us acquire just such an imagination — without a trace of the soft sentimentality and without compromising an inch of evangelical conviction."

That last part of Peterson's endorsement -- "without compromising an inch of evangelical conviction" -- I find very difficult to understand. As a seasoned (read "old") theologian, I have major issues with Bell's evangelical conviction and believe his 200-page broadside should be taken seriously.[2] *Christianity Today* recently quoted Peterson as saying, "There's very little Christ, very little Jesus, in these people who are fighting Rob Bell."[3]

My desire in this book is not to "fight Bell," but to carefully evaluate the doctrine he is presenting and to respond to the charge that we Evangelicals have hijacked the Jesus story.

Christian leaders have the responsibility of testing all things and holding fast to that which is good (I Thes. 5:21). There is a <u>faith</u>, a content of truth, which we need to understand, enjoy, and defend (Jude 3). We are commanded in I Timothy 4 to "Watch your life and doctrine closely. Persevere in them, because if you do, you will save both yourself and your hearers." (v. 16). *Love Wins* is not a work of poetry or a fictional essay, but rather is a theological treatise intended to challenge the prevailing viewpoint among Evangelical Christians. It is our duty to understand *Love Wins* and to respond to it charitably and biblically.

Should you read *Love Wins*? Absolutely, <u>if</u> you are a seasoned follower of Jesus Christ and have a measure of theological discernment.[4] If you are a new believer in Christ, read it with another believer who will help you see Bell's errors in understanding Scripture, his theological aberrations, and his seductive use of well-worded questions.[5] The back cover of *Love Wins*, by the way, has the text:

"'God loves us.
God offers us everlasting life by grace, freely,
through no merit on our part.
Unless you do not respond the right way.
Then God will torture you forever.
In hell.'
Huh?"

—
2

The purpose of this book is to help church leaders and serious Christians understand where Bell is coming from. Those who have read *Love Wins* will hopefully be encouraged by this evaluation of his attack on hell to stand strong for the "once-for-all-delivered-to-the-saints'- faith" (Jude 3). Those who have not read or do not intend to read *Love Wins* will be asked by others about Bell and his viewpoint. This book will provide a brief, biblical response to his book.

Who Is Rob Bell and Why Should I Care?

He is the pastor of a large church in Michigan, Mars Hill Bible Church, and a graduate of Wheaton and Fuller Seminary. He is probably best known for his NOOMA video series[6] and has authored several other books, including *Velvet Elvis* and *Sex God* and is the co-author of *Jesus Wants to Save Christians*. Every believer is charged with defending the faith and, if you read his book, you will see that a number of key doctrines are being called into question. That's why you should care.

Some Positive Points:

First, I'm grateful for the massive issue that Rob Bell has dealt with in his book. Can there be a larger topic than "the fate of every person who ever lived"? The subject of one's eternal destiny cannot be trumped by any other issue.

One is reminded of the Master Questioner Jesus who asked in Matthew 16:26- "What good will it be for someone to gain the whole world, yet forfeit their soul? Or what can anyone give in exchange for their soul?" Apparently, according to Jesus, one can forfeit his soul for this world. Of course, in dealing with this most vital of questions, if Bell is wrong, the potential for deceiving many is great. A.W. Tozer put it well when he said, "The vague and tenuous hope that God is too kind to punish the ungodly has become a deadly opiate for the consciences of millions."

Atheist Robert Ingersoll rejected the idea of a place of eternal torment. On one occasion, after he had delivered a fervent refutation of the doctrine, assuring his audience that every respected intellectual had dismissed the idea of hell, a drunk approached him and said, "Bob, I liked your lecture; I liked what you said about hell. But, Bob, I want you to be sure about it, because I'm depending on you."[7] If Bell is wrong, his is not a better story, but a misleading story.[8]

Second, I appreciate Bell's passion, especially for those who have been turned off by poor representatives of Christ who have argued for the eternal lostness of *others* -- and seemed glad about it.[9] Callous conservatism is antithetical to the heart of the gospel. The challenge of TRUTH + LOVE is a hard balance to achieve, but one that we dare not duck (Eph. 4:15).

Third, I'm also thankful for some of the pictures he paints of the abundant life in Christ that can be lived now and later enjoyed eternally. He's done a good job of attacking an other-worldly gospel that ignores the plight of this world and focuses only on somewhere *else.* He writes, "Life has never been about just 'getting in,' It's about triving in God's good world. It's stillness, peace, and that feeling of your soul being at rest, while at the same time it's about asking things, learning things, creating things, and sharing it all with others who are finding the same kind of joy in the same good world." (179). Although I believe he sometimes overstates his case, Bell is right that many believers focus too much of their attention on getting there instead of asking how we can bring heaven down here.

However, in spite of these positive comments, we must carefully evaluate the theology of Bell's book. In doing so we want to be marked by a critical mind, but not by a critical spirit. There is a middle way between the extremes of being gullible and being hypercritical -- and that middle way is a careful, biblical evaluation of a position. None of us should engage in Bell-bashing.

Bell's Universalistic-Sounding Arguments:[10]

The promotional video for Bell's book incited Evangelical bloggers to post comments challenging his apparent universalism. For some it might be helpful to read the full transcript of that video:

"Several years ago we had an art show at our church and people brought in all kinds of sculptures and paintings, and they put them on display. And there was this one piece that had a quote from Ghandi in it. And lots of people found this piece compelling. They'd stop and sort of stare at it and take it in and reflect on it. But not everyone found it that compelling. Somewhere in the course of the art show, somebody attached a handwritten note to the piece and on the note they had written: 'Reality check. He's in hell!' Ghandi's in hell? He is? And someone knows this for sure? And felt the need to let the rest of us know? Will only a few select people make it to heaven? And will billions and billions of people burn forever in hell? And if that's the case -- how do you become one of the few? Is it what you believe, or what you say, or what you do, or who you know, or something that happens in your heart? Or do you need to be initiated or baptized or take a class or be converted or be born again? How does one become one of these 'few'? And then there is the question behind the questions. The real question: What is God like? Because millions and millions of people were taught that the primary message, the center of the gospel of Jesus, is that God is going to send you to hell unless you believe in Jesus. And so what gets suddenly sort of caught and taught is that Jesus rescues you from God. But what kind of God is that that we would need to be rescued from this God? How could that God ever be good? How could that God ever be trusted? And how could that ever be 'good news'? This is why lots of people want nothing to do with the Christian faith. They see it as an endless list of absurdities and inconsistencies and they say,

'Why would I ever want to be a part of that?' See, what we believe about heaven and hell is incredibly important because it exposes what we believe about who God is and what God is like. What you discover in the Bible is so surprising unexpectantly beautiful that whatever we've been told or taught, the Good News is actually better than that! Better than we could ever imagine. The Good News is that LOVE WINS!"[11]

In his earlier work *Velvet Elvis*, Bell tells the story of taking his family out to dinner. Asking for the check, the waitress tells him that someone had already paid his bill. There was nothing left for him to pay. Bell implies that this story illustrates something very significant about the saving work of Jesus Christ. He writes, "So this reality, this forgiveness, this reconciliation, is true for everybody. Paul insisted that when Jesus died on the cross, he was reconciling 'all things, in heaven and on earth, to God.' All things, everywhere. This reality then isn't something that we make true about ourselves by doing something. It is already true. Our choice is to live in this new reality or cling to a reality of our own making." (*Velvet Elvis*, p. 146).[12]

He has also written in *Velvet Elvis*: "Heaven is full of forgiven people. Hell is full of forgiven people. Heaven is full of people God loves, whom Jesus died for. Hell is full of forgiven people God loves, whom Jesus died for. The difference is how we choose to live, which story we choose to live in, which version of reality we trust. Ours or God's." (*Velvet Elvis*, p. 146).[13]

Inside and Outside:

This perspective sounds very much like Karl Barth's universalism where he says, "Jesus Christ is God's mighty command to open our eyes and to realize that this place is all around us, that we are already in this kingdom, that we have no alternative but to adjust ourselves to it, that we have our being and continuance here and nowhere else. In Him we are already there, we already belong to it. To enter at His command is to realise that in Him we are already inside."[14]

Barth's "inside" language seems quite the opposite of Jesus' "outside" language, doesn't it? We read in Matthew 8:12 where Jesus says, "But the subjects of the kingdom will be thrown <u>outside</u>, into the darkness, where there will be weeping and gnashing of teeth." In Matthew 22:13, Jesus says, "Then the king told the attendants, 'Tie him hand and foot, and throw him <u>outside</u>, into the darkness, where there will be weeping and gnashing of teeth.' Jesus also says in Matthew 25:30: "And throw that worthless servant <u>outside</u>, into he darkness, where there will be weeping and gnashing of teeth.'" He also taught in Mark 4:11 that "The secret of the kingdom of God has been given to you. But to those on the <u>outside</u> everything is said in parables."

Throughout *Love Wins* Bell seems to argue for the belief that all without exception will be saved. For example, he states that the Sodom and Gomorrah story is actually a story of a hope of redemption for all (83-85). He writes,

> No matter how painful, brutal, oppressive, no matter how far people find themselves from home because of their sin, indifference, and rejection, there's always the assurance that it won't be this way forever. (86)

He advocates a remedial, rather than a retributive, view of hell.[15] "Failure, we see again and again, isn't final, judgment has a point, and consequences are for correction." (88). Nothing is said by Bell about God's wrath in his book.[16]

Speaking of the lost coin, sheep, and son in Luke 15, Bell says, "The God that Jesus teaches us about doesn't give up until everything that was lost is found. This God simply doesn't give up. Ever." (101). The possibility of eternally resisting God's love isn't entertained by Bell. This runs counter to Jesus' lament in Matthew

23: "Jerusalem, Jerusalem, you who kill the prophets and stone those sent to you, how often I have longed to gather your children together, as a hen gathers her chicks under her wings, and you were not willing." (Mt. 23:37). The parable of the rich man and Lazarus in Luke 16 seems clearly to imply that the rich man resisted God's love. It is a massive leap in logic (as well as contradictory to the "great chasm [which] has been fixed" in verse 26) to suggest that one day the rich man will cross over into heaven.

An Inflammatory Question:

Bell asks the question, "Have billions of people been created only to spend eternity in conscious punishment and torment, suffering infinitely for the finite sins they committed in the few years they spent on earth? . . . in the end, will God give up?" (102). Before we deal with his question of infinite punishment for finite sin, did you notice how his first question was worded? The question implies that such eternally-condemned people were created by God specifically to be tormented and that those people have never had a chance to turn to Christ.

A god who would create billions of innocent people for the sole purpose of torturing them forever would certainly be an ogre, would he not? Is that the picture of the God of the Bible? Is that really the story Evangelicals are telling of the Triune God? If not, then Bell has set up a straw man. Evangelicals steadfastly affirm Genesis 18:25 which asks, "Will not the Judge of all the earth do right?" Bell seems to actually believe that Evangelicals hold to the idea that "billions of people [have] been created only to spend eternity in conscious punishment and torment." Bell's implication is that those billions condemned by the message of Evangelicals are innocent, unfairly treated by God, and of no value whatsoever.

Part of the problem here is a minimization of sin. If Uzzah in the Old Testament could instantly be struck down in death for touching the ark of God (2 Sam. 6), and Ananias and Sapphira could be executed for lying to the Holy Spirit (Acts 5), how much greater judgment will be on those who reject His Son? The writer of Hebrews puts it this way: "How much severer punishment do you think he will deserve who has trampled under foot the Son of God, and has regarded as unclean the blood of the covenant by which he was sanctified, and has insulted the Spirit of grace?" (Heb. 10:29).

Infinite Judgment for Finite Sins?

This argument against infinite judgment for finite sins is an old one.[17] The traditional view of eternal punishment seems incompatible with God's justice, some say. The argument is that sins consciously committed in time do not seem to merit conscious torment throughout eternity. Pinnock said, "I consider the concept of hell as endless torment in body and mind an outrageous doctrine, a theological and moral enormity." To inflict infinite suffering upon those who have committed finite sins, as Pinnock argues, would go far beyond an eye for an eye and a tooth for a tooth. There would be a serious disproportion between sins committed in time and the suffering upon those who have committed finite sins, as Pinnock argues, would go far beyond an eye for an eye and a tooth for a tooth. There would be a serious disproportion between sins committed in time and the suffering experienced forever. The fact that sin has been committed against an infinite God does not make the sin infinite. The chief point is that eternal torment serves no purpose and exhibits a vindictiveness out of keeping with the love of God revealed in the gospel."

However, that viewpoint also rules out annihilationism, doesn't it? Annihilation is certainly eternal in its effect. How can eternally wiping a person out of existence be reconciled with his or her temporal sins?

9

Two Errors:

There are at least two mistakes in the viewpoint which says that infinite punishment does not fit finite sin. The first is that such a position assumes that the seriousness of a sin is directly related to the time it takes to commit it. But murder might take only a few minutes to commit, while a robbery might take hours.

Second, the critical issue is the person against whom the sin is committed. To steal from a stranger is bad, but stealing from one's mother is even more serious because one owes greater respect to one's parents. If one takes into account the nature of sin as well as the person against whom the sin is committed, one might ask, "How much more serious, then, is even the slightest offense against an absolutely holy God, who is worthy of our com- plete and perpetual allegiance? Indeed, sin against an absolutely holy God is absolutely serious. For this reason, the unredeemed suffer absolute, unending alienation from God; this alienation is the essence of hell. It is the annihilationist's theory that is morally flawed. Their God is not truly holy, for he does not demand that sin receive its due."[18]

Eternal Persuasion?

Bell also argues that ". . . there are others who [are] . . . trusting that there will be endless opportunities in an endless amount of time for people to say yes to God. As long as it takes, in other words." (106-107). The implication here, of course, is that time is the issue. God needs to use eternity to persuade, cajole, or compel all sinners to see things God's way and repent, according to this viewpoint. Barclay put this way: "It is a question of God using an eternity of persuasion and appeal until the hardest heart breaks down and the most stubborn sinner repents."[19]

But what about the issue of human freedom? The universalist Ferré emphasizes that "ultimately God's freedom and man's belong together; and man's freedom to be over-against God is not the freedom to remain an eternal problem child. God's creation and pedagogy are both too good for that!"[20] Ferré says, "A terrible thing is hell . . . in the long run, beyond our understanding, but the God who loves us will never be mocked by our stubborn depth of freedom, but for our sakes will put on the screws tighter and tighter until we come to ourselves and are willing to consider the good which He has prepared for us."[21] Philip Gulley says that before he became a universalist, "I defended our freedom to reject God but denied God's freedom to reject our rejection."[22]

One writer says, "The advocates of universal restoration are commonly the most strenuous defenders of the inalienable freedom of the human will to make choices contrary to its past character and to all the motives which are or can be brought to bear upon it. As a matter of fact, we find in this world that men choose sin in spite of infinite motives to the contrary. Upon the theory of human freedom just mentioned, no motives which God can use will certainly accomplish the salvation of all moral creatures. The soul which resists Christ here may resist him forever."[23] Later we will deal with Bell's poor view of death, for the teaching of the Scriptures is that death ends all opportunities of salvation.[24]

Bell writes, ". . . given enough time, everybody will turn to God and find themselves in the joy and peace of God's presence. The love of God will melt every hard heart, and even the most 'depraved sinners' will eventually give up their resistance and turn to God." (107). The NT scholar C.H. Dodd said, "As every human being lies under God's judgment, so every human being is ultimately destined, in His mercy, to eternal life." The implications, of course, are that this life does not provide sufficient opportunity for God to "melt every hard heart," that the only equation possible is SINNER + ETERNITY = REDEMPTION.

There is not a shred of evidence in the Scriptures that sinners will repent in the after-death state. I have an old King James Bible which has as the paragraph title for Luke 16:19-31 (the story of the rich man and Lazarus), "A Soul Repents in Hell." Bad paragraph title! For the story of the rich man and Lazarus in Luke 16 indicates that the rich man, in torment in hell, engages not in repentance, but in recrimination.[25]

Nels F.S. Ferré wrote that "Traditional orthodoxy has to be challenged, fought and slain."[26] He continues, "Not to believe in full consummation insults the character of God or sells the power of Christ short." In another place he says that "The logic of the situation is simple. Either God could not or would not save all. If He could not He is not sovereign; then not all things are possible with God. If He would not, again the New Testament is wrong, for it openly claims that He would have all to be saved. Nor would He be totally good."[27] So one must sacrifice either God's omnipotence or His goodness to hold to the possibility of even one sinner being lost forever.

One wonders if Bell has been reading Dodd or Ferré when he writes, "Within this proper, larger understanding of just what the Jesus story even is, we see that Jesus himself, again and again, demonstrates how seriously he takes his role in saving and rescuing and redeeming not just everything, but everybody." (150-151). Later he asserts, "What Jesus does is declare that he, and he alone, is saving everybody." (155).

The Narrow Road:

What is Bell's understanding of Matthew 7:13-14, a key passage he does not discuss in *Love Wins*?

> 13 "Enter through the narrow gate. For wide is the gate and broad is the road that leads to destruction, and many enter through it. 14 But small is the gate and narrow the road that leads to life, and only a few find it."

This text is difficult to argue around, and it is not surprising that Bell does not deal with it. The gate is described as "narrow" and "small" that leads to life. But the gate and road that lead to destruction are described as "wide" and "broad." In terms of sheer numbers, there are "many" that enter destruction through that wide gate and broad road. "Only a few" find the small gate and the narrow road that lead to life. We suspect -- and here we are speculating -- that Bell would agree that some go into a kind of temporary destruction, but certainly not for eternity.

A Prodigal Interpretation:

Bell uses the story of the prodigal son in Luke 15 to prove two points: first, that it is a story of integration, not separation (169-170). However, the biblical text itself indicates that Jesus told the parable to reveal the Father's heart toward sinners. We read in verse 2, "But the Pharisees and the teachers of the law muttered, 'This man welcomes sinners and eats with them.'" The religious leaders of Israel did not have the Father's heart, and so criticized Jesus for reaching out to sinners. The story itself shows a disgusted older brother who doesn't lift a finger to search for his younger, wayward sibling, and is ticked when the father welcomes the prodigal home. The story certainly sounds like a story of separation (the older brother separates himself from his prodigal brother and from his celebratory father).

Bell understands the story to teach that both the prodigal son who went away and the elder brother who stayed were both in the family, but the latter simply refused to join in the party.[28] Hell is of his own making. Bell implies that the older brother is in heaven; he's just sitting in a corner sulking. Bell's interpretation of Luke 16 stands in contrast with Jesus often stating that the religious leaders will find themselves outside God's kingdom.

Bell then makes a second point from Luke 16 and says, "The father's love cannot be earned, and it cannot be taken away. It just is." (187). He further says, "Our trusting, our change of heart, our believing God's version of our story doesn't bring it into existence, make it happen, or create it. It simply is." (188). These statements imply that believing the gospel has no transactional effect upon the sinner, that belief is immaterial to the reality of being in the Father's love.[29]

The Cry of Forgiveness at Calvary:

Referring to Christ's statement on the cross of "Father, forgive them, for they do not know what they are doing," Bell says, "Jesus forgives them all, without their asking for it. Done. Taken care of.[30] Before we could be good enough or right enough, before we could even believe the right things." (189).[31] Please notice that again Bell disparages belief, arguing that the reality of forgive- ness applies to all even without their asking for it. How unlike human forgiveness Bell's position is. On a human level, forgiveness must be accepted, responded to, received, to be realized. One is not surprised that Bell discourages conversations intended to lead to conversions.

Bell refers to I Timothy 2:4's statement that God wants all people to be saved and to come to a knowledge of the truth. This expression of God's will leads him to a series of questions. In Chapter 4, entitled "Does God Get What God Wants?", Bell asks, "Can one really believe that God doesn't get what He wants?" "Will all people be saved, or will God not get what God wants?" (98). "In the Bible, God is not helpless, God is not powerless, and God is not impotent." (101). "Will 'all the ends of the earth' come, as God has decided, or only some? Will all feast as it's promised in Psalm 22, or only a few? Will everybody be given a new heart, or only a limited number of people? Will God, in the end, settle, saying, 'Well, I tried. I gave it my best shot, and sometimes you just have to be okay with failure'? Will God shrug God-size shoulders and say, 'You can't always get what you want'?" (103).

God's very greatness is dependent on whether God gets what God wants. He writes: "How great is God? Great enough to achieve what God sets out to do, or kind of great, medium great, great most of the time, but in this, the fate of billions of people, not totally great. Sort of great. A little great." (97-98). If challenging the greatness of God is not blasphemy, then I am hard-pressed to define the term.

God's Two Wills:

Bell is obviously missing the biblical perspective of what some theologians call the two wills of God. Some use the terms "permissive" (what God allows) and "perfect" (what God desires). When we read in I Thessalonians 4 that "It is God's will that you should be sanctified: that you should avoid sexual immorality; that each of you should learn to control your own body in a way that is holy and honorable . . ." (verses 3-4), does God always get what God wants? No. Even Christians fall into immorality. Do their sins compromise the greatness of God? Of course not. Bell has taken I Timothy 2:4 in a most absolute sense of God's having to save every human being without exception. If He does not save every human being, His very greatness is called into question.

God Is Not Great?

The idea of tying God's greatness to the necessity of His saving everyone is not a new one. John A.T. Robinson put it this way: "[T]he truth of universalism is not the peripheral topic of speculation for which it has often been taken. If God is what ultimately He asserts Himself to be, then how He vindicates Himself as God and the nature of His final lordship is at the same time the answer to what He essentially is. The truth or falsity of the universalistic assertion, that in the end He is Lord entirely of a world wanting His lordship, is consequently decisive for the whole Christian doctrine of God."[32]

15

Nels F.S. Ferré tries to make a similar point when he says, "Some have never really seen how completely contradictory are heaven and hell as eternal realities. Their eyes have never been opened to this truth. If eternal hell is real, love is eternally frustrated and heaven is a place of mourning and concern for the lost. Such joy and such grief cannot go together. There can be no psychiatric split personality for the real lovers of God and surely not for God himself. That is the reason that heaven can be heaven only when it has emptied hell, as surely as love is love and God is God. God cannot be faithless to Himself no matter how faithless we are; and His is the power, the kingdom and the glory."[33] In Ferré's view, not saving all means not only that God is not great, but that He suffers from a psychiatric condition!

How foolish to connect the very nature and being and greatness of God solely to His saving work! Robert Jeffress responds to the comment that God must save all if He is to save any by writing, ". . . imagine that the president of the United States pardons an individual from death row due to extenuating circumstances surrounding the case. Some may not agree with the president's decision, but does anyone accuse him of being unmerciful because he did not pardon every prisoner on death row? The fact that he pardoned one person is evidence of the president's compassion, not cruelty."[34] He was under no obligation to save any. Such an anthropocentric approach undermines the grace of God, making God man's debtor.

T hree Options:

Based on our survey so far in *Love Wins*, it may be helpful to remind ourselves that there are really only three options (discussed in Christianity) when it comes to the eternal fate of the wicked:

1. annihilationism: This view is sometimes called "conditional immortality" and teaches that the wicked will be put out of existence. (Sadly, John R.W. Stott sided with this perspective in his book Evangelical Essentials).

2. universalism: This perspective teaches that all will eventually be saved, either in this life or in the world to come (some even include the devil and the demonic world among those who will be redeemed).[35]

3. eternal conscious punishment: This perspective teaches that a second category of human beings will continue to exist, separated from God and God's people, for ever.

Bell has to fit into one of these categories, doesn't he? Throughout *Love Wins* he attacks with vehemence the 3rd view (eternal conscious punishment) and repeatedly states that Jesus will save all. Logically he fits into category #2.

B ell's "Escape" Clauses:

To be fair, there are several places where he seems to deny universalism -- as he has in some interviews. He says, "Love demands freedom. It always has, and it always will. We are free to resist, reject, and rebel against God's ways for us. We can have all the hell we want." (113). This statement is found ironically in Chapter 4 which is entitled "Does God Get What God Wants?"

It appears that the hell Bell believes in is here, on this earth. No one will go to an eternal hell in his theology. I suspect that when he denies being a universalist, he is referring to one who thinks God will forcibly sweep all into heaven against their will. Bell's universalism is more subtle and seems to incorporate a willing acceptance of the gospel on the part of the sinner after (perhaps) eons of God's working on the sinner's hard heart.

ⓄO rigen as Orthodox?

Bell appears to be an inconsistent universalist, arguing for that viewpoint as a legitimate one in Christian history.[36] He suggests that universalism is one option among others in the stream of Christian belief. But defined in its broadest terms, "the stream of Christian belief" could include Arianism, Gnosticism, Docetism, etc.

Bell is not alone in claiming that universalism and Christianity are not incompatible. There are those who call themselves Christian universalists (or CU's) or even Evangelical universalists (EU's). These are represented by books such as *If Grace Is True: Why God Will Save Every Person* by Philip Gulley and James Mulholland, *The Inescapable Love of God* by Thomas Talbott, and even the book with the oxymoronic title *The Evangelical Universalist* by Gregory MacDonald (a pseudonym using the first name from Gregory of Nyssa, an early universalist, and MacDonald, from George MacDonald, a universalist who had a great impact on the writings of C.S. Lewis).

In *If Grace Is True: Why God Will Save Every Person*, Gulley argues that he used to believe in the eternal conscious punishment view, but he has now found a "much better gospel." He says that this better gospel teaches that God will save everybody. But how does he know that this new message is true?

Gulley, a Quaker by tradition, says the following about the Scriptures:

"God doesn't restrict his communication to the Bible." (19)
"But I need to admit my faith is not based primarily on theological reasoning. I believe because God whispered in my ear." (18).
"These experiences with God have become the bedrock of my faith. I trust them." (21).

He admits that his new view (of universalism) is contrary to the Word of God: "How could I justify what ran counter to certain Scriptures?" (22).

"I had . . . been taught a set of beliefs and an interpretation of Scripture that required the damnation of those who did not believe as I believed. . . . [Peter's story of his call to preach the gospel to the Gentiles] encouraged me to base my faith on my experiences with God." (26).

"I am also grateful I've been freed from my need to confine God within the boundaries of my tradition and my interpretations of Scripture." (26).

"The Bible was never intended to end the conversation, but to encourage it." (37).

We must believe in a "God of fresh words" (continuing revelation) (40).

"I used to believe the Bible was the ultimate solution of authority. In so doing, I elevated Scripture to a status equal with God. . . . When I lifted up the Bible as my ultimate authority, I made my leather-bound, gold-engraved Bible into a paper calf." (42).

"If you believe every statement or story about God recorded in Scripture is equally true, nothing I can say will alter your conviction that God will save some and damn the rest." (49)

How does Gulley know that his new viewpoint is correct? He answers, "God whispered in my ear."[37]

Talbott (in his *The Inescapable Love of God*) discusses 2 Thessalonians 1:8-9 where we read, "8 He will punish those who do not know God and do not obey the gospel of our Lord Jesus. 9 They will be punished with everlasting destruction and shut out from the presence of the Lord and from the glory of his might . . ."

Talbott argues that even this clearest-sounding text for eternal conscious punishment can be explained away redemptively if one will "only use one's theological imagination"!

19

He writes, "For nothing works greater mischief in theology, I am persuaded, than a simple failure of the imagination, the inability to put things together in imaginative ways."[38] I submit there is something which works greater mischief in theology and so it's called unbelief. I'm reminded of William Horton's comment (as he reviewed Love Wins): "Where Scripture has clearly spoken, Bell has not wrestled sufficiently. Yet where Scripture is silent, he unleashes his imagination."[39]

The Evangelical Universalist argues that God's love will win all, even if it takes eons to convince sinners of the need of the gospel.

H ow Should We Respond?

Should Christians want to see people condemned eternally? Of course not! But we affirm that people need to hear the gospel and believe the gospel to be saved. We find no biblical evidence that there will be opportunities to respond to Christ after death.[40]

The bigger question, far more important than where Bell stands, is this: Is universalism justified biblically? We take passages like the following which rule out universalism very seriously.

> "It is appointed unto men once to die, but after this the judgment" (Heb. 9:27).
> Jesus said, "If you do not believe that I am he, you will indeed die in your sins." (Jn. 8:24).
> "Whoever believes in the Son has eternal life, but whoever rejects the Son will not see life, for God's wrath remains on them." (Jn. 3:36).
> In His parable of the sheep and the goats, Jesus said, "Then they [the goats] will go away to eternal punishment, but the righteous [the sheep] to eternal life." (Mt. 25:46).

There is no doubt that other texts emphasize the cruciality of repenting and believing the gospel in this life. Jesus tells the story of the wealthy farmer whose crops were blessed and he began planning to expand his business. As he poured over the most recent John Deere tractor catalogues, he heard a voice which said, 20"You fool! This very night your life will be demanded from you. Then who will get what you have prepared for yourself?" (Lk. 12). In Luke 13 Jesus makes it quite clear that one must be prepared to meet God. Vicious crimes and violent accidents happen to God's people, so they should be ready (vv. 1-5). The story of the rich man and Lazarus clearly indicates that the rich man (traditionally called "Dives," Latin for "rich man") went to a place of agony and torment upon his death, could not escape that fate, and that a great chasm was fixed between him and heaven (Lk. 16:19-31). This passage clearly conforms to other Scriptures about the intermediate state (that time period between one's death and one's bodily resurrection).

Gutting Missions

One must ask the question, why should Christians go to other countries, learn difficult foreign languages and cultures, and eat what human beings were never intended to eat, if all will eventually be saved? Southeastern Baptist Theological Seminary President Daniel Akin, on Twitter, said, "If theological inclusivism & hypothetical universalism is true [then] any rationale for missions is gutted. Why go? They do not need the gospel."[41]

In his excellent review of Bell's book, Kevin DeYoung writes,

According to Bell, salvation is realizing you're already saved. We are all forgiven. We are all loved, equally and fully by God who has made peace with everyone . . . Bell is saying God has already forgiven us whether we ask for it or not, whether we repent and believe or not, whether we are born again or not . . . Bell categorically rejects any notion of penal

---

substitution. It simply does not work in his system or with his view of God . . . At the very heart of this controversy . . . is that we really do have two different Gods. The stakes are that high. If Bell is right, then historic orthodoxy is toxic and terrible. But if the traditional view of heaven and hell are right, Bell is blaspheming. I do not use the word lightly, just like Bell probably chose "toxic" quite deliberately. Both sides cannot be right.[42]

How are we to respond to Rob Bell? There seems to be abundant evidence to describe him as a false teacher, a well-intentioned, sincere, engaging, hip, compassionate wolf in sheep's clothing. The Apostle Paul warned the Ephesian elders about such teachers in Acts 20 when he said:

28 Keep watch over yourselves and all the flock of which the Holy Spirit has made you overseers. Be shepherds of the church of God, which he bought with his own blood. 29 I know that after I leave, savage wolves will come in among you and will not spare the flock. 30 Even from your own number men will arise and distort the truth in order to draw away disciples after them. 31 So be on your guard! Remember that for three years I never stopped warning each of you night and day with tears.

Several points occur to me from this text. First, we should not be surprised when "savage wolves," homegrown wolves, come in among God's people and have no intention of sparing the flock. What makes us think that we are better protected or more special than the First Century believers from false teachers and those who would proclaim "another gospel" (see Gal. 1:8)?[43]

We have an obligation to the Holy Spirit of God who has made us leaders among God's people to protect them. We are to "be on our guard" against those who distort the truth and seek to draw disciples after them.

Our response to such attacks should not be vitriol or anger, but tears and grief that the Good News about Christ is being twisted.

If I have understood Bell correctly, he stands very clearly in the line of universalists like Karl Barth, C.H. Dodd, John A.T. Robinson, Nels F.S. Ferré, Thomas Talbott, Philip Gulley, and perhaps even Bishop Carlton Pearson.[44] Everybody is already redeemed; the price has been paid for all. Our obligation is not to produce converts, but to convince all that they are already in the family of God. If there even is a hell, it is temporary, remedial, and of man's own making. The very idea that Jesus came to rescue us from God and His holiness is repugnant to Bell. This cannot be described any other way than another gospel.

We were told at the beginning of this book that we Evangelicals are toxic hijackers. A hijacker puts the lives of others in grave danger, attempting to take what does not belong to him. It would seem to me that Bell has taken on the role of hijacker and that his substitute gospel puts many in grave danger of thinking that they are automatically in the family of God or that they will have an eternity of opportunities to choose Christ. He is attempting to take what does not belong to him, the one and only gospel which saves.

Appendix #1: Faith As Instrumental Cause of Salvation:

We must respond to Bell's oft-repeated minimization of belief. Referring to Christ's statement on the cross of "Father, forgive them, for they do not know what they are doing," Bell says, "Jesus forgives them all, without their asking for it. Done. Taken care of. Before we could be good enough or right enough, before we could even believe the right things." (189)

He writes, "So this reality, this forgiveness, this reconciliation, is true for everybody. Paul insisted that when Jesus died on the cross, he was reconciling 'all things, in heaven and on earth, to God.' All things, every- where. This reality then isn't something that we make true about ourselves by doing something. It is already true. Our choice is to live in this new reality or cling to a reality of our own making." (*Velvet Elvis*, p. 146).

But let's notice just from the gospel of John how absolutely crucial personal faith is. Here is a listing of most of the references to belief or faith in the fourth gospel:

> John came as a witness to testify to the light, "so that through him all men might believe." (1:7).
> "to all who received him, to those who believed in his name, he gave the right to become children of God . . ." (1:12).
> "He thus revealed his glory, and his disciples put their faith in him." (2:11)."
> After he was raised from the dead, his disciples recalled what he had said. Then they believed the Scripture and the words that Jesus had spoken." (2:22).
> ". . . many people saw the miraculous signs he was doing and believed in his name." (2:23).

"I have spoken to you of earthly things and you do not believe; how then will you believe if I speak of heavenly things?" (3:12).

"Just as Moses lifted up the snake in the desert, so the Son of Man must be lifted up, that everyone who believes in him may have eternal life." (3:15).

"For God so loved the world that he gave his one and only Son, that whoever believes in him shall not perish but have eternal life." (3:16).

"Whoever believes in him is not condemned, but whoever does not believe stands condemned already because he has not believed in the name of God's one and only Son." (3:18).

"Whoever believes in the Son has eternal life, but whoever rejects the Son will not see life, for God's wrath remains on him." (3:36).

"Many of the Samaritans from that town believed in him because of the woman's testimony, 'He told me everything I ever did.'" (4:39)

"And because of his words many more became believers." (4:41).

"They said to the woman, 'We no longer believe just because of what you said; now we have heard for ourselves, and we know that this man really is the Savior of the world.'" (4:42).

"'Unless you people see miraculous signs and wonders,' Jesus told him, 'you will never believe.'" (4:48).

". . . So he and all his household believed." (4:53).

"'I tell you the truth, whoever hears my word and believes him who sent me has eternal life and will not be condemned; he has crossed over from death to life.'" (5:24).

"'. . . nor does his word dwell in you, for you do not believe the one he sent.'" (5:38).

"'If you believed Moses, you would believe me, for he wrote about me. But since you do not believe what he wrote, how are you going to believe what I say?'" (5:46-47).

"'Do not work for food that spoils, but for food that endures to eternal life, which the Son of Man will give you. On him God the Father has placed his seal of approval.'

They they asked him, 'What must we do to do the works God requires?' Jesus answered, 'The work of God is this: to believe in the one he has sent.'" (6:27-29).

"'For my Father's will is that everyone who looks to the Son and believes in him shall have eternal life, and I will raise him up at the last day.'" (6:40).

"'I tell you the truth, he who believes has everlasting life.'" (6:47).

"'Whoever believes in me, as the Scripture has said, streams of living water will flow from within him.'" (7:38).

"'Has any of the rulers or the Pharisees believed in him?'" (7:48).

"'I told you that you would die in your sins; if you do not believe that I am the one I claim to be, you will indeed die in your sins.'" (8:24).

"Jesus heard that they had thrown him out, and when he found him, he said, 'Do you believe in the Son of Man?' . . . 'Lord, I believe,' and he worshiped him." (9:35, 38).

"'Do not believe me unless I do what my Father does. But if I do it, even though you do not believe me, believe the miracles, that you may know and understand that the Father is in me, and I in the Father.'" (10:37-38).

"And in that place many believed in Jesus." (10:42).

"'. . . for your sake I am glad I was not there, so that you may believe.'" (11:15).

"Jesus said to her, 'I am the resurrection and the life. He who believes in me will live, even though he dies; and whoever lives and believes in me will never die.'" (11:25-26).

"Therefore many of the Jews who had come to visit Mary, and had seen what Jesus did, put their faith in him." (11:45).

"[F]or on account of him [Lazarus] many of the Jews were going over to Jesus and putting their faith in him." (12:11).

"'Put your trust in the light while you have it, so that you may become sons of light.'" (12:36).

"Yet at the same time many even among the leaders believed in him. But because of the Pharisees they would "not confess their faith for fear they would be put out of the synagogue; for they loved praise from men more than praise from God." (12:42-43).

"'Do not let your hearts be troubled. Trust in God; trust also in me.'" (14:1).

"'Believe me when I say that I am in the Father and the Father is in me; or at least believe on the evidence of the miracles themselves.'" (14:11).

"'7 But very truly I tell you, it is for your good that I am going away. Unless I go away, the Advocate will not come to you; but if I go, I will send him to you. 8 When he comes, he will prove the world to be in the wrong about sin and righteousness and judgment: 9 about sin, because people do not believe in me; 10 about righteousness, because I am going to the Father, where you can see me no longer; 11 and about judgment, because the prince of this world now stands condemned.'" (16:7-11).

20 "'My prayer is not for them alone. I pray also for those who will believe in me through their message, that all of them may be one, Father, just as you are in me and I am in you. May they also be in us so that the world may believe that you have sent me.'" (17:20-21).

"27 Then he said to Thomas, "Put your finger here; see my hands. Reach out your hand and put it into my side. Stop doubting and believe."
28 Thomas said to him, "My Lord and my God!" 29 Then Jesus told him, "Because you have seen me, you have believed; blessed are those who have not seen and yet have believed." 30 Jesus performed many other signs in the presence of his disciples, which are not recorded in this book. 31 But these are written that you may believe that Jesus is the Messiah, the Son of God, and that by believing you may have life in his name." (20:27-31).

Here are several **clear conclusions** which can be drawn from these texts:
1. Not all people will believe in this life (1:7).
2. To those who believe they are given the right to become children of God (1:12).
3. Belief often happens in response to evidence (2:22-23; 4:48; 10:37-38; 11:15; 14:11; 20:27-31).
4. Eternal life is promised to those who believe in Him as well as their own resurrection (3:15, 36; 6:40, 47; 20:31)
5. Those who believe are guaranteed not to perish nor be condemned, but have crossed over from death to life (3:16, 18; 5:24). Those who believe in him will never die (11:25-26).
6. Those who do not believe or reject the Son won't see life and will have God's wrath remaining on him (3:36). They will also die in their sins (8:24).
7. The work of God is to believe in the one he has sent (6:29).
8. Sometimes belief is described as "going over to Jesus and putting their faith in him" (11:45; 12:11).
9. Jesus demands the same faith in himself as the disciples had in God (14:1).
10. It is sin not to believe in Jesus and the Holy Spirit convicts men of that sin (16:7-11).

---

11. The unity of God's people should lead to the world believing that God sent the Son (17:20-21).

12. The fourth gospel was written to drive people to put their faith in Jesus that by believing they might have life in His name (20:27-31).

It seems to me that a viewpoint which demeans personal faith in Christ while arguing that people will have an eternity to believe the gospel is contradicted by the fourth gospel in no uncertain terms.

𝔸 ppendix #2: A Biblical Doctrine of Death As Ending All Opportunities for Salvation

Bell provides no Scriptural support for his contention that people will have endless opportunities after death to respond to the gospel. I'm reminded of the late Donald Bloesch who said, "We do not wish to build fences around God's grace . . . and we do not preclude the possibility that some in hell might finally be translated into heaven."[45] The open theist John Sanders put it this way: "Those who assert the possibility of a future chance do not make death the decisive barrier of time for people to make a decision of faith."[46]

Many Scriptures indicate that this life is absolutely crucial for believing the gospel. The Lord Himself emphasizes that between those in hell and those in heaven there is a "great gulf fixed, so that those who want to pass from here to you cannot, nor can those from there pass to us"? (Luke 16:26, NKJV) A chasm, rather than merely a fence, is the biblical image here.

Those who die without trusting Him, Jesus says, are like an astute farmer who built bigger barns but forgot the unpredictable inevitability of death and ignored the fate of his soul (Luke 12:13-21).

The late Canadian novelist Robertson Davies once prayed, "Oh God, don't let me die stupid!" For those who buy into Bell's gospel, thinking that they will have eons to trust in Jesus post-mortem, they are dying stupid.

Appendix #3: Jesus on Judgment in the Gospel of Matthew

In interviews, Bell has recoiled from the idea that he doesn't believe in hell. He says, "I have a whole chapter devoted to that topic." He briefly covers the less than a dozen places where Jesus uses the term "hell" and says, "That's it. That's all the times the word is used."

But one could ask, how many times must God Incarnate speak of a subject for it to be considered important? He has greatly under-valued Jesus' teaching on eternal lostness.

Bertrand Russell rejected Christianity and Jesus Christ mainly because of the doctrine of hell. He wrote, "There is one very serious defect to my mind in Christ's moral character, and that is that He believed in hell. I do not myself feel that any person who is really profoundly humane can believe in everlasting punishment."[47] The Unitarian minister Theodore Parker once remarked: "I believe that Jesus Christ taught eternal punishment — I do not accept it on his authority!"

It is abundantly clear from the following passages in Matthew's gospel (where the term "hell" is not used) that Jesus spoke the most about eternal judgment.

Some Points in Matthew's Gospel on
Eternal Lostness Missed by Bell:

1. Jesus speaks of "the danger of the fire of hell" (Mt. 5:22) and of being "condemned to hell" (Mt. 23:33).
2. Jesus speaks of the narrow gate & the broad way (Mt. 7:13-14).

3. Jesus says that many will demand to be let into heaven at the end of time and He will say, "I never knew you. Away from me, you evildoers!" The entrance requirement for heaven is a personal relationship with Jesus Christ (Mt. 7:23; 25:10-12).

4. Jesus says that those who thought they were guaranteed the kingdom "will be thrown outside, into the darkness, where there will be weeping and gnashing of teeth." They will not throw themselves out; they will be thrown. (Mt. 8:10-12; 18:6-9).

5. Jesus says that the demons believe a time of torturing is coming (Mt. 8:28-29; 18:32-35).

6. Jesus says there will be differences of punishment in hell (Mt. 10:15; 11:20-24).

7. Jesus says we should be afraid of the One who can destroy both soul and body in hell (Mt. 10:28).

8. Jesus speaks of disowning in heaven those who disown Him in this life (Mt. 10:32).

9. Jesus speaks of the unforgivable sin against the Holy Spirit -- a sin that will not be forgiven in the age to come (Mt. 12:30-32).

10. Jesus speaks of harvest time at the end of the world in which the weeds will be separated from the wheat (and will be burned) and the bad fish will be separated from the good fish (and will be thrown away). "The angels will come and separate the wicked from the righteous and throw them into the blazing furnace, where there will be weeping and gnashing of teeth." (Mt. 13:30-50).

11. Jesus says there will be some who will seek to gain the whole world, but will forfeit their soul (Mt. 16:24-27).

12. Jesus says those who show up at the wedding feast without the proper clothes will be bound and thrown "outside, into the darkness, where there will be weeping and gnashing of teeth." (Mt. 22:11-14; 25:29-30).

13. Jesus says that His angels "will gather his elect from the four winds" (Mt. 24:31). [Barth makes all of humanity the elect].

31

14.   Jesus says all of humanity will be divided into two groups: the sheep who knew the Lord and showed it by their works and the goats who did not know the Lord and did not meet the needs of others. The goats "will go away to eternal punishment, but the righteous (the sheep) to eternal life." (Mt. 25:46).

15.   Jesus commands His followers to fulfill the Great Commission and to "make disciples of all nations." (Mt. 28:19-20).

Appendix #4: A Brief Study on the Wrath of God

Bell criticizes a church's website which speaks of eternal judgment in their doctrinal statement. He remarks, "Welcome to our church!" But if a church believes in hell, shouldn't it say so?

I checked Mars Hill Bible Church's website for their statement on eternal lostness and found the following:

> We believe the day is coming when Jesus will return to judge the world, bringing an end to injustice and restoring all things to God's original intent. God will reclaim this world and rule forever. The earth's groaning will cease and God will dwell with us here in a restored creation. On that day we will beat swords into tools for cultivating the earth, the wolf will lie down with the lamb, there will be no more death, and God will wipe away all our tears. Our relationships with God, others, ourselves, and creation will be whole. All will flourish as God intends. This is what we long for. This is what we hope for. And we are giving our lives to living out that future reality now.[48]

It seems to me that there is a logic of damnation that Christians have not fully explored. D.A. Carson puts it this way:

Hell is not a place where people are consigned because they were pretty good blokes but just didn't believe the right stuff. They're consigned there, first and foremost, because they defy their Maker and want to be at the center of the universe. Hell is not filled with people who have already repented, only God isn't gentle enough or good enough to let them out. It's filled with people who, for all eternity, still want to be at the center of the universe and who persist in their God-defying rebellion. What is God to do? If he says it doesn't matter to him, then God is no longer a God to be admired. He's either amoral or positively creepy. For him to act in any other way in the face of such blatant defiance would be to reduce God himself.[49]

In light of Bell's complete absence of speaking of God's wrath, I have inserted below my article on that topic from a number of years ago. Hopefully, you will find it helpful:

"Warning a Wrath-Deserving World:
Evangelicals and the Overhaul of Hell"
By Larry Dixon[50]

"Hell is Manhattan at rush hour!", stated the occasional theologian Woody Allen. No doubt his viewpoint has changed over the last year; perhaps he would now agree with Sartre that hell is other people—or himself.

The Anglican pop theologian Tom Harpur (in his best seller *Life After Death*), attacks the idea of hell as,

> so naive that the average thinking person can easily conclude the whole subject is one for children and for lovers of pure fantasy . . . . There are few ideas

in the entire history of religion that have caused more misery, cruelty and misunderstanding than the concept of a fiery hell.[51]

Thomas Talbott argues that a God who can send humans to hell is "an altogether pagan conception of God."[52] Another writer confesses that for many Christians, "Hell is like a dirty little secret that rears its nasty head at inappropriate moments."[53] Hell is deeply unfashionable, says Charles Pickstone. He suggests that "the disappear- ance of hell in the twentieth century is not because hell is no longer believed in—rather it is suppressed, blocked off. It is too close for comfort."[54] But is it really?

If we evangelicals are serious about developing plans for reaching the contemporary world for Christ, our strategizing must include the biblical doctrine of judgment. We are not free to pick and choose the beliefs which please us and then call that system biblical Christianity. For if mere desire eliminated judgment, none of us would have to be concerned about a holy God. John A. T. Robinson gave voice to this sentiment when he wrote that:

> We live, in the twentieth century, in a world without judgment, a world where at the last frontier post you simply go out—and nothing happens. It is like coming to the customs and finding there are none after all. And the suspicion that this is in fact the case spreads fast: for it is what we should all like to believe. [55]

Evangelicalism is not unanimous in wanting to defend the biblical doctrine of judgment, however. One theologian argues that "it is . . . likely that this monstrous belief [in the traditional view of hell as eternal conscious punishment] will cause many people to turn away from Christianity, that it will hurt and not help our evangelism."[56] I believe Gomes is right when he argues that "the rejection of eternal punishment is but one incident in the larger campaign to construct a kinder, gentler theology."[57] Referred to as "theology's H-word" (Newsweek), hell has been described as an "odious conception, . . . blasphemous in its view of the Creator" (Sir Arthur Conan Doyle), as "an outrageous doctrine, a theological and moral enormity" (Clark H. Pinnock), and as "the final mockery of God's nature" (John A. T. Robinson). Timothy Phillips seeks to rally the evangelical troops when he writes that "historically speaking, the time is ripe for a new conservative reaction to this mockery and damnation of hell."[58]

The Apostle Paul proclaims that "we are to God the aroma of Christ among those who are being saved and those who are perishing. To the one we are the smell of death; to the other, the fragrance of life. And who is equal to such a task?" (2 Cor. 2:15-16). A brief look at the evangelical landscape indicates that we often choose to turn away from such a task, preferring to be thought of as a fragrance, rather than a stench, to our culture.

Shifting metaphors, Henri Nouwen suggests that:

> The basic question is whether we ministers of Jesus Christ have not already been so deeply molded by the seductive power of our dark world that we have become blind to our own and other people's fatal state and have lost our power and motivation to swim for our lives.[59]

Rather than serving as vigilant lifeguards who clearly and convincingly scream "SHARK!", we believers seem to prefer the role of Son-bathers on vacation.

Several evangelical leaders are back-peddling[60] on the issue
of judgment, as the following scenario illustrates:

One Sunday night as you meet with other Christians to hear
a sermon on the end times, the featured speaker reads the
following quotation to emphasize a point about God's
judgment:

> How can Christians possibly project a deity of such
> cruelty and vindictiveness whose ways include
> inflicting everlasting torture upon his creatures,
> however sinful they may have been? Surely a God
> who would do such a thing is more nearly like Satan
> than like God, at least by any ordinary moral
> standards, and by the Gospel itself.

Is he quoting from some cultic tract written by a Jehovah's
Witness? No, he is simply using a statement from the well-
known Canadian evangelical Clark H. Pinnock.[61]

A week later you are in your car listening to a cassette of a
debate between a liberal Anglican bishop and a noted British
evangelical writer. You hear one of them say:

> I . . . believe that the ultimate annihilation of the
> wicked should at least be accepted as a legitimate,
> biblically-founded alternative to their eternal,
> conscious torment. . . .

> [Christians should] survey afresh the biblical material
> [and reject the doctrine of eternal conscious
> punishment].

Which of the two theologians made that statement? Was it the liberal David Edwards? No, you discover that the well-respected senior statesman of evangelical Christianity, John R. W. Stott, is the source of that challenge.[62]

Visiting a church in Iowa the next weekend, you hear a professor of theology proclaim that "We do not wish to build fences around God's grace . . . and we do not preclude the possibility that some in hell might finally be translated into heaven." Asking someone after the service, you learn that the man who made that unbiblical declaration was not from a liberal denomination or some New Age support group, but the popular evangelical writer Donald Bloesch.[63]

Hoping your luck will change, you drive to Canada to hear the influential British evangelical Michael Green defend biblical Christianity to a university crowd. He does an excellent job as he proclaims Christ's relevance to 20th century North Americans.

Buying his book *Evangelism Through the Local Church* at the book table after the meeting, you read Green's rhetorical question on page 69:

> What sort of God would he be who could rejoice eternally in heaven with the saved, while downstairs the cries of the lost make an agonizing cacophony? Such a God is not the person revealed in Scripture as utterly just and utterly loving.[64]

In that same book Green describes the God of Christians who still hold to the doctrine of the eternal punishment of the wicked as a "Cosmic Torturer."[65]

What are Christians to say when such important evangelical leaders express their "overhaul" of hell? These are not statements taken out of context; some of these men have written extensively of their personal pilgrimage away from the traditional understanding of final judgment. Moreover, several invite fellow evangelicals to turn away from that basic Christian doctrine, offering their reformulated views as supposedly more biblical substitutes.

Other examples of back-peddling could be mentioned: The late F.F. Bruce, perhaps the foremost New Testament scholar which evangelicalism has produced, wrote a complimentary foreword[66] to Edward Fudge's promotion of annihilationism (*The Fire Which Consumes*). Fudge's book was offered as an alternate selection of the Evangelical Club several years ago, and a flyer expressing "loving concern" promoted his book at a discount to the ETS mailing list.

At the 1989 Evangelical Affirmations Conference held at Trinity Evangelical Divinity School, the Statement of Affirmations drawn up by those key scholars and pastors in the evangelical movement purposely omitted a more specific stand concerning the fate of the wicked than the official statement that "unbelievers will be separated eternally from God." Crafting a more detailed position was not an oversight. After a plea by a young Adventist in the last plenary session, a straw vote of the 500 or so invitees reflected an almost 60% agreement not to include a specific position on the doctrine of hell.

What has happened to the doctrine of hell? James Davison Hunter surveyed a number of Bible College and seminary students several years ago and discovered that,

Evangelicals generally and the coming generation particularly have adopted to various degrees an ethical code of political civility. This compels them not only to be tolerant of others' beliefs, opinions, and life-styles, but more importantly to be tolerable to others. The critical dogma is not to offend but to be genteel and civil in social relations. . . . [Such] a religious style . . . entails a deemphasis of Evangelicalism's more offensive aspects, such as accusations of heresy, sin, immorality, and paganism, and themes of judgment, divine wrath, damnation, and hell.[67]

Truly, the servant is not greater than his master, nor the student than his teacher. When evangelical leaders slip doctrinally, we are quick to criticize and even condemn. But when was the last time you heard a sermon on hell? Or, if you are a pastor, preached one? Lest any of us feel we are off the hook, when was the last time we thanked God for rescuing us from His righteous wrath? I am sure I have chosen to water-down my presentation of the gospel to unbelievers at times by purposely not mentioning God's judgment and hell—haven't you? When we communicate the gospel of Jesus Christ only as a means to peace and happiness, already peaceful and happy pagans will politely listen and then turn away. We should not be surprised that a sin-numbed and self-deceived world will only shrug its shoulders and yawn at a gospel message whittled away to only "peace and happiness in Jesus." Today's evangelicals need to be reminded of the urgency of escaping God's judgment. And it is a simple truth that "if the house is burning or the ship is sinking, you do not whisper 'Fire' or 'Mayday'; you shout it!"[68]

Could it be that we are not so sure anymore that our world is under the wrath of God? Perhaps the very expression, "a wrath-deserving world," offends us, causes us to cringe, embarrasses us. In 1990 the Roman Catholic Auxiliary

Bishop Austin Vaughan warned New York's Governor Mario Cuomo that his abortion position was putting him in danger of hell. That pronouncement seemed archaic, almost quaint to a society whose sole sense of hell is its use as a worn-out expletive. But is it only pro-abortion, power-wielding politicians who are candidates for eternal condemnation?

Two hundred and fifty years ago Jonathan Edwards was not reluctant to preach his "Sinners in the Hands of an Angry God" sermon, relentlessly concentrating on the mage of hell-fire. It might not hurt us to note several examples of his challenge to that congregation:

> There is nothing that keeps wicked men at any one moment out of hell, but the mere pleasure of God.

> [Divine] justice calls aloud for an infinite punishment of [the wicked's] sins.

> The wrath of God burns against them, their damnation does not slumber; the pit is prepared, the fire is made ready, the furnace is now hot, ready to receive them; the flames do now rage and glow. The glittering sword is whet, and held over them, and the pit hath opened its mouth under them.

> There are in the souls of wicked men those hellish principles reigning, that would presently kindle and flame out into hell-fire, if it were not for God's restraints.

> There is laid in the very nature of carnal men, a foundation for the torments of hell.

God has laid himself under no obligation, by any promise to keep any natural man out of hell one moment.

The devil is waiting for them, hell is gaping for them, the flames gather and flash about them, and would fain lay hold on them, and swallow them up; the fire bent up in their own hearts is struggling to break out; and they have no interest in any Mediator, there are no means within reach that can be any security to them. In short, they have no refuge, nothing to take hold of; all that preserves them every moment is the mere arbitrary will, and uncovenanted, unobliged forbearance of an incensed God.

Your wickedness makes you as it were heavy as lead, and to tend downwards with great weight and pressure towards hell; and if God should let you go, you would immediately sink and swiftly descend and plunge into the bottomless gulf . . . All your righteousness, would have no more influence to uphold you and keep you out of hell, than a spider's web would have to stop a fallen rock.

Describing God's wrath as a dreadful storm, as dam waters that can no longer be held back, and as a flood of God's vengeance, Edwards then takes up a hunting image:

The bow of God's wrath is bent and the arrow made ready on the string, and justice bends the arrow at your heart, and strains the bow, and it is nothing but the mere pleasure of God, and that of an angry God, without any promise or obligation at all, that keeps the arrow one moment from being made drunk with your blood.[69]

Speaking of God's "mere" mercy, Edwards says to this Connecticut congregation in 1741:

> It is to be ascribed to nothing else, that you did not go to hell the last night; that you was [sic] suffered to awake again in this world, after you closed your eyes to sleep. And there is no other reason to be given, why you have not dropped into hell since you arose in the morning, but that God's hand has held you up.[70]

But Edwards does not leave this congregation dangling over the pit; he proceeds to invite them to turn to Christ:

> Now you have an extraordinary opportunity, a day wherein Christ has thrown the door of mercy wide open, and stands in calling and crying with a loud voice to poor sinners; a day wherein many are flocking to him, and pressing into the kingdom of God.[71]

His sermon concludes with the invitation: "Therefore, let every one that is out of Christ, now awake and fly from the wrath to come."[72]

But Edwards' sermon is not unanimously held in high regard by those who profess to be evangelicals. Clark Pinnock dismisses Edwards as one who had "cauterized [his] conscience" to believe in and preach the traditional doctrine of hell. He then caricatures Edwards by saying that "reading Edwards gives one the impression of people watching a cat trapped in a microwave squirm in agony, while taking delight in it."[73] Such an understanding of the gospel, Pinnock argues, is nothing more than "sadism raised to new levels of finesse."[74] Pinnock challenges such an approach, arguing that for such people "hell is the ultimate big stick to threaten people with."[75]

But R. C. Sproul rightly defends Edwards when he reminds us that "a sadist who believed in hell would probably be more likely to give assurances to people that they were in no danger of hell, so that he could deliciously relish the contemplation of their falling into it."[76] Edwards was no sadist, but a biblical realist who wished to be faithful to the teaching of Scripture.

Today's society would certainly like to change Edwards' sermon to "God in the Hands of Angry Sinners", for the prevailing opinion is that we live not in a wrath-deserving world, but an explanation-, even apology-demanding world, where the Creator, not the creature, is in the dock.

Rather than being warned about the fear of hell, people today want to be talked, not threatened, into the kingdom of God. However, fear can be an excellent motivator when the danger is legitimate and lethal. A person camping in Arizona who hears an eerie rattling sound near his sleeping bag does not dissertate on the relative merits of a decision reached out of fear; he flees from the heart-terrorizing sounds of a diamond-back! We resent fear as a motivator when it seems manipulative and artificial, but when there is a real and present danger, fear can be a powerful kick-start to a right decision! Paul argues this point in 2 Corinthians 5 when he writes: "Since, then, we know what it is to fear the Lord, we try to persuade men" (2 Cor. 5:11). Similarly, the writer to the Hebrews asserts that "it is a fearful thing to fall into the hands of the living God" (Heb. 10:31, AV).

The gospel means "good news", but it is not just good news. Edith Schaeffer reminds us,

43

The powerful voice of God warns of judgment, and the same voice expresses His compassion for those who come back to Him in His given way. We are to listen with the same intensity of awe we feel when we observe the power of water. His spoken truth is not for us to judge or edit; we are to listen, absorb, understand, and bow.[77]

When we move away from the biblical description of our righteous condemnation by a holy God, we edit the bad news of the good news. All evangelicals would acknowledge that a compromise of the good news of the gospel (for example, arguing that one must add his own good works to Christ's sacrifice in order to be saved) is a very serious error. However, some act as if the bad news of the good news is open to private interpretation, or may be revised in the light of what is considered "morally repulsive and logically nonsensical,"[78] or may be adjusted or altered for public consumption, or may simply be overlooked as a theological unmentionable.

One preacher said that when we present the truth about Christ and pagans do not get angry, either they did not understand or we did not say it right! We should not seek to alienate unbelievers, but we should also not attempt to highlight only the "good" points of the gospel.

We evangelicals must return to a biblical and responsible apocalypticism which taps into the feeling that "culturally, a sense of the end is as much in the air as carbon monoxide in Los Angeles."[79] We need to recapture the concept of God's holy wrath—and warn people of judgment. Daniel Fuller poignantly comments:

> How terrible it would be at the judgment day to see
> people condemned because, while we had taught them
> parts of the biblical message, we had said little or
> nothing about hell! . . . We please God when we warn
> people about hell, even though such preaching can
> incur anger and ridicule.[80]

Rescue from God's righteous and eternal wrath, we believe, is
one of the best parts of the gospel! Although we are told three
times in the book of Ezekiel that "God takes no delight in the
death of the wicked" (18:23, 32; 33:11), that same book warns
again and again of the wrath of God. "Wrath is upon the whole
crowd," Ezekiel declares (7:12). God's wrath is something to
be "spent" (13:15), "poured out" (21:31), and "blown" upon
sinners (22:21). God says, "I will pour out my wrath on them
and consume them with my fiery anger, bringing down on their
own heads all they have done" (22:31). God speaks of His
"zeal and holy wrath" (38:19).

Other Scriptures teach us that the Lord is One who is
"provoked to wrath" (Deut. 9:7), that the wicked sometimes "stir
up more of His wrath" (Neh. 13:18), and that "the desire of the
righteous ends only in good, but the hope of the wicked only in
wrath" (Prov. 11:23). Isaiah warns that "the day of the Lord is
coming—a cruel day, with wrath and fierce anger—to make the
land desolate and destroy the sinners within it" (Isa. 13:9).

The prophet Nahum declares that "the Lord is a jealous and
avenging God; the Lord takes vengeance and is filled with
wrath. The Lord takes vengeance on his foes and maintains
his wrath against his enemies" (Nah. 1:2).

John the Baptist's message was to "flee from the coming
wrath" (Matt. 3:7). The Apostle Paul argues that the wicked
are "storing up wrath against [themselves] for the day of God's
wrath" (Rom. 2:5). The concept of God's avenging wrath is

---

not an embarrassment to Paul, for he admonishes the Roman believers with the words: "Do not take revenge, my friends, but leave room for God's wrath, for it is written: 'It is mine to avenge; I will repay,' says the Lord" (Rom. 12:19).

Certain theologies, it seems, provide precious little room for God's wrath. But believers in Christ should see themselves as those who once "were by nature objects of wrath" (Eph. 2:3). Paul praises God for His mercy, emphasizing the truth that "God did not appoint us to suffer wrath but to receive salvation" (1 Thes. 5:9). Fuller is correct when he states that

> The basic problem with Pinnock's objection [to the traditional view of hell] is that he does not probe deeply enough into the reason why God sent his Son to die for sinners. He certainly did it because he loved them, but why did this love mean that his Son had to die for them? The scriptural answer is that Christ came to die "as the one who would turn aside [God's] wrath" (Rom. 3:25 margin). Jesus had to appease God's anger so that God would remain just when he forgave sinners and in no wise tarnish his own glory. "He [sent Christ to die] . . . so as to be just and the one who justifies those who have faith in Jesus" (Rom. 3:26).[81]

The Bible teaches that God's wrath is presently restrained. Isaiah 48:9 records the Lord saying that "For my own name's sake I delay my wrath." But His wrath will not be interminably delayed. Colossians 3:6 says that "the wrath of God is coming" and Revelation 6:17 declares that "the great day of their wrath [both the Father's and the Son's] has come, and who can stand?"

God's wrath, however, is not seen in Scripture as a solely future event. John 3:36 declares that "Whoever rejects the Son will not see life, for God's wrath remains on him." Timothy Phillips sees this text as a problem for annihilationists, for "as long as God's wrath abides on them, the damned must exist."[82]

Condemnation has already been declared, as Jesus makes clear earlier in that same chapter: "Whoever does not believe stands condemned already" (John 3:18b). Our world does not need to hear wild predictions about future judgment, but clear declarations about the unbeliever's present condition before a holy God.

The prevailing opinion among many unbelievers, as one writer expressed it, is that "God may not even be, but if He is, one thing is sure, He could not send anyone to hell even if He wanted to. His mercy has His hands of holy wrath tied behind His back."[83] However, such a sentiment does not seem to be confined to "unbelievers."

Some evangelicals are backing away from the concept of God's eschatological, everlasting wrath, preferring to interpret hell in terms of remedial, rather than retributive, punishment. In this understanding, hell will be a school.

The liberal Nels F. S. Ferré argues that "Beyond earthly life lies the larger school where we are expected to mature according to new conditions."[84] In another place, he says,

> A terrible thing is hell . . . in the long run, beyond our understanding, but the God who loves us will never be mocked by our stubborn depth of freedom, but for our sakes will put on the screws tighter and tighter until we come to ourselves and are willing to consider the good which He has prepared for us.[85]

47

Millard Erickson's comment of a few years ago that it is "difficult to find any evangelicals" who hold to universalism[86] is no longer accurate. I know of one such evangelical universalist in the ranks of the Evangelical Theological Society. His position is that hell will provide God sufficient opportunities to convince the unbeliever to see things God's way.

But such an approach (that hell will be a school in which all eventually come to repentance) is misguided and unbiblical. Contrary to the opinion of some, Scripture gives no indication that there will be repentance in hell, for "the reprobate will be petrified in their wickedness."[87] Perhaps the theological debate between *poena damni* and *poena sensus* has contributed to the hope that the wicked might eventually be able to escape hell.[88]

Someone has argued that "hell is truth seen too late." I would disagree and argue that hell is truth twisted and hurled in the face of God. The "repentance" of Dives in Luke 16 is just the opposite: he blames God for being insufficiently warned himself about hell, and insists that his brothers would repent if someone came back from the dead, arguing that they do not have enough evidence for repentance in the five books of Moses (vv. 30-31)! His attitude is recrimination, not repentance!

In studying the terms for God's wrath, William Crockett concludes that the most serious term used by Paul for wrath "expresses the utter hopelessness of the wicked in the face of an angry God":

[Paul] chooses this term to underscore the fact that in the eschaton rebellious sinners have no hope of salvation. They will be taken from the presence of God and the righteous and placed, in effect, beyond the pale of God's love. The righteous go the way of life, the wicked the way of death.[89]

Phillips aptly asks: "Isn't the hope that God would eternally pursue the unregenerate a reflection of man's refusal to accept the eternal consequences of his own sin?"[90] Pinnock, on the other hand, argues that eschatological wrath "is a factor not to be excluded, although it should not dominate the picture."[91]

John Stott states that "we need to remember that God is the Creator of all humankind, and remains infinitely loving, patient and compassionate towards all whom he has made."[92] However, as Crockett argues:

[Eschatological *orgē* is genuine anger devoid of love. In Paul's theology eschatological wrath means that after death God no longer loves the wicked, nor is He prepared to act on behalf of the wicked . . . . Rather, his [Eschatological *orgē* is genuine anger devoid of love. In Paul's theology eschatological wrath means that after death God no longer loves the wicked, nor is He prepared to act on behalf of the wicked . . . . Rather, he separates the righteous from the wicked. There is no meaningful way to say that God loves the wicked after death.[93]

Therefore, contra Stott, God does not remain infinitely loving; there are limits to His love. One day the "door" to salvation will be shut (Luke 13:25); there will come a time when it will be "too late" for salvation (Luke 12:35-48); the day of grace will end,

---

49

and there will be a resurrection of some "to everlasting life, others to shame and everlasting contempt" (Dan. 12:2).

One should not be embarrassed to testify that he or she came to faith in Christ primarily in order to escape hell. As I have tried to demonstrate elsewhere, the major source for our doctrine of hell is the Good Shepherd Himself.[94] This difficult doctrine of hell refuses to be confined to semester-ending discussions of eschatology, for its reality impinges on other areas such as theology proper, anthropology, and soteriology. Phillips is again correct, I believe, when he states that "Every alternative to hell calls into question Christ's work. Nothing less than the person and work of Jesus Christ is at stake in the doctrine of hell."[95]

A few Christians will react to the evangelical overhaul of hell positively, glad that they no longer have to hold to what one liberal theologian calls "the fantasy of the fanatical." Others will re-examine the Scriptures, especially the teachings of the Lord Jesus Himself, and will be reminded that the horror of hell is remedied only by the crime at Calvary. They will realize that revisions of the penalty for sin necessarily affect one's view of the price paid to redeem sinners.

Some human beings will unfortunately insist with William Ernest Henley that:
> It matters not how strait the gate,
> How charged with punishments the scroll,
> I am the master of my fate:
> I am the captain of my soul.[96]

For those who choose the way of death we grieve. But we must not water-down the biblical description of such a decision's eternal consequences.

We agree with John Gerstner when he writes that "the fear of hell is the only thing most likely to get worldly people thinking about the Kingdom of God. No rational human being can be convinced that he is in imminent danger of everlasting torment and do nothing about it!"[97]

ppendix #5: Should Bell and *Love Wins* Be a Litmus Test of Orthodoxy?

Mark Galli, senior managing editor of *Christianity Today*, editorialized on May 5, 2011, in an article entitled "Rob Bell Is Not a Litmus Test: What One Thinks about *Love Wins* Is No Test of Faith."[98] Galli's thoughts produced the following points of response:

Galli believes the idea that Bell is becoming a litmus test of orthodoxy is "silly" and Evangelicals should swim against the current of thinking that he is a test of orthodoxy. When I was a student in biology class in high school, I learned that a litmus test in chemistry is a test "to establish the acidity or alkalinity of a mixture." All I remember of those days is that a piece of paper could be dipped into some chemical and turn a certain color (I don't recall which color indicated what). A second definition of a "litmus test" is that it provides "a critical indication of future success or failure." It seems to me that Bell and *Love Wins* are indeed a litmus test about certain doctrines. How can they not be? His book is not intended as fiction, but rather as a theological revision to what most Evangelicals believe. Furthermore, "silly" would not be the word I would have used! I'm not sure that calling the discussion silly really helps Christians get very serious about theology.

He compares *Love Wins* to *The Shack*, emphasizing that Christians have not held Young's strange views of the Trinity (he lapses into modalism, for example) against him. Galli writes, "We recognize that an author trying to repeat the old, old story in fresh ways will sometimes overstep the bounds of traditional theology." This is quite different than what Bell is seeking to

51

do in *Love Wins*. Bell makes it very clear that he disagrees with the "old, old story"; that Evangelicals have hijacked that story, having replaced it with a "toxic" story of their own.

Galli writes that Bell "loves Jesus. He wants to see lots of people come to believe in Jesus. He wants to see the world transformed in Jesus' name. He really thinks the Bible is a book through which Jesus speaks authoritatively. He believes in miracles. He believes Jesus is coming again." Not to put too fine a point on it, but those same statements could be made about most Jehovah's Witnesses and even Mormons that I've met! I'm not saying that Bell isn't a true believer. But the fact that he is a brother makes him more accountable for his teaching, not less. Let's assume for a moment that Bell is a wolf in sheep's clothing. Would he not appear to be one who loves Jesus? One who "wants to see lots of people come to believe in Jesus? [One who] wants to see the world transformed in Jesus' name? [One who] really thinks the Bible is a book through which Jesus speaks authoritatively? [One who] believes in miracles? [One who] believes Jesus is coming again"?

Has Galli watched Bell's Nooma video "Bullhorn" in which he mocks a "brother in Christ" who is trying to (imperfectly) share the gospel with genuinely lost people?

Galli suggests that "we have no choice in this day but to listen to and respond charitably to ideas we had thought were settled long ago, ideas that make us feel uncomfortable, ideas that seem to threaten our faith." He says we should be beyond name-calling, that "we live in a time when we must engage afresh all these permutations of orthodoxy, heterodoxy, heresy, paganism, and apostasy." I'm not sure that our time is all that unique (Galli may be suffering from a bit of "chronological snobbery," as C.S. Lewis called it. Nor am I sure the internet age really qualifies as a new era in church history). Serious Christians have not confined their theological defenses to name-calling, I don't believe.

Galli further argues "That means we're going to have to get used to some card carrying evangelicals experimenting with ideas that centrists, like me anyway, consider less than helpful." First of all, I'm not sure Bell wants to be known as a card-carrying evangelical. He has publicly stated that if his views get him kicked out of the E-club, he's okay with that. And some theological positions ought to cause some "evangelicals" to hand over their cards.

Galli says, "Very few people present a new way of conceiving a doctrine unless they are trying to solve a genuine problem in the church." Some people present a new way of conceiving a doctrine simply because they don't like what the Bible really teaches (see our examples of universalists in this paper).

Galli says, "In *Love Wins*, Bell reinterprets some biblical themes (e.g., last judgment, atonement) because he believes the way we've traditionally talked about these themes is not faithful to the Bible and pushes people away from Jesus. I think he's right that the way we've talked about substitutionary atonement and hell have hardly been biblical much of the time, and thus these doctrines have caused more problems than they have solved." Wow. I'd really like to know what Galli is referring to here. Most Evangelical churches I know speak very little about hell. What does Galli mean by the charge that the way we've talked about substitutionary atonement and hell "have hardly been biblical much of the time"? What does he mean that "these doctrines have caused more problems than they have solved"? Bell doesn't favor the penal-substitutionary view of the atonement and says nothing about God's wrath.

Galli says that the fact "that Bell offers a decidedly minority view, doesn't make Bell a heretic, though he may be unbiblical at points." The term "heresy" comes from a word meaning choice --

and I think Bell has made his choice. He's been wooed over to an inconsistent form of universalism and he's on the attack in *Love Wins*. Should Bell be brought up on heresy charges? No, if the bad news of the gospel is unclear and ambiguous. No, if people don't have to believe the gospel before they die. No, if the death of Christ automatically reconciled all without exception to God, whether they believe or not. [I actually thought about contacting Bell's elders at his church to challenge them to hold him responsible for his unbiblical teaching, but then I read their doctrinal statement].

Galli makes the point that "the fact that so many resonate with Bell's concerns about these themes means we need to wrestle with them afresh." People have always "wrestled" with the biblical doctrine of hell. If churches are teaching the whole counsel of God, then they will thoroughly discuss the doctrine of eternal lostness.

If Bell's book is not a test of orthodoxy, what <u>would</u> be, in Galli's opinion?

---

[1] This, of course, was the message tweeted by Pastor John Piper when he heard of Bell's book. I've discussed Piper's apparently sarcastic dismissal of Bell in my blog: http://larrydixon.wordpress.com/ The blog is entitled: "A Little Bit of Sarcasm: Piper Needs No Defending."

[2] I am quite puzzled by Mark Galli's article entitled "Rob Bell Is Not a Litmus Test: What one thinks about *Love Wins* is no test of orthodoxy" in *Christianity Today*, May 5, 2011. We will discuss Galli's article in our last appendix.

[3] *Christianity Today*, May, 2011, p. 19, section entitled "Quotation Marks".

[4] As a seminary professor, I often recommend to my students what I call "books that will boil your blood before you get past the preface." Such books are not for spiritual nourishment, but for making us aware of the arguments of those who reject Christianity. Some of those boiling books on my list include: *Farewell to God* (Charles Templeton), *A Heretic's Guide to Eternity* (Spencer Burke), and my lapsed friend Brian McLaren's *The Last Word and the Word after That.*

[5] Bell's questions (someone estimated that there are 350 of them in this book) are not innocent. They are well-constructed, often visceral, challenges to orthodox beliefs. Todd Magnum makes the excellent point that they are frequently little more than examples of *reductio ad absurdum*. See his review of Bell's book at: http://www.biblical.edu/images/stories/academics/forms/lovewinsmangumrev iew.pdf

---

6 His *Nooma* video entitled "Bullhorn," produced back in 2005, criticizes an open air preacher for warning people to flee from God's wrath and is strangely prescient of this 2011 book, *Love Wins.*

7 Quoted in Robert Jeffress, *Hell? Yes!* (Waterbrook Press, 2004), p. 73.

8 I identify with the comment made by Thomas Howard (in an article about "The Parts Angels Play") when he writes that "The Bible is the Book with the story in it. You have to follow how the author tells his story. You have to stick with his own emphases. You cannot go tooting off to write your own story and then call it his."

9 I'm told of the comment by one wag who said, "The gospel ain't important unless someone around here can get *damned*!" In over forty years of ministry, I've yet to meet someone who seemed glad about anyone facing eternal punishment.

10 We will be citing earlier universalists who have made the same points that Bell is repeating about universal salvation. See chapter 2 of *The Other Side of the Good News* for a full discussion of universalists such as Origen, Karl Barth, C.H. Dodd, John A.T. Robinson, Nels F.S. Ferré , and Thomas Talbott.

11 Bell's promo video (a brilliant piece of marketing by HarperOne) can be found here: www.youtube.com/watch?v=ODUvw2McL8g The Bayly brothers produced a parody video of Bell's promo that is grab-your-sides-hilarious (in my opinion). See it at: http://www.baylyblog.com/2011/04/rob-bells-department-of-silly-talks.html

12 This, of course, raises the very important question of personal faith. Does belief make something true? What is the role of believing the gospel? We will examine this issue in-depth at the end of this book .

13 One is reminded of the Tennessee grandmother Mary Baxter's statement in her book *A Divine Revelation of Hell* that "Though those in hell were lost forever, I knew that He still loved them and would for all eternity." (New Kensington, PA: Whitaker House, 1993, p. 37). Quoted in Larry Dixon, *Heaven: Thinking Now about Forever* (Christian Publications, 2002, p. 59). This viewpoint runs counter to the biblical idea that those who die without Christ are under God's wrath forever (John 3:36; see also Dan. 12:2 which speaks of a resurrection of others to "shame and everlasting contempt").

14 *Church Dogmatics*, vol. 4, part I, pp. 99-100. Quoted in *The Other Side of the Good News*, p. 41. Barth continues by saying, "Man has already been put in the place and kingdom of peace with God . . . His decision and act, therefore, can consist only in obedience to the fact that he begins and does not cease to breathe in this place and kingdom, that he follows the decision already made and the act already accomplished by God, confirming them in his own human decision and act; that he, for his part, chooses what has already been chosen and actualized for him." (Ibid. p. 100).

15 A "remedial" view suggests that God's punishment will bring repentance and change. A "retributive" view teaches that God's punishment is rightfully-deserved wrath without the possibility of repentance. See my article, "Warning a Wrath-Deserving World: Evangelicals and the Overhaul of Hell," *The Emmaus* Journal, 2:7-21, Summer 1993, for a fuller discussion.

16 Bell assumes that the doctrine of eternal conscious punishment has no point. The contemporary universalist Thomas Talbott argues that the term

"punishment" refers only to remedial, not retributive, punishment. He cites the well-respected commentator William Barclay to support his contention but fails to mention that Barclay was himself committed to universalism and that the term "punishment" does sometimes carry the sense of divine retribution and revenge (see William Lane Craig's articles in http://www.leaderu.com/offices/billcraig/docs/talbott1.html).

17 We deal with this argument as articulated by the late annihilationist Clark Pinnock on pp. 100-103 and p. 189 of our *The Other Side of the Good News*.

18 Alan W. Gomes, "Evangelicals and Hell, Part Two," *Christian Research Journal* (Summer 1991), p. 9.

19 William Barclay, *A Spiritual Autobiography* (Grand Rapids: Eerdmans, 1977), p. 68.

20 Nels F.S. Ferré, *The Christian Understanding of God* (London: SCM Press, 1951), p. 237.

21 Ibid., p. 240.

22 *If Grace Is True*, p. 109.

23 *The Other Side of the Good News*, p. 61. Statement is found in Harry Friesen, "A Critical Analysis of Universalism" (Th.D. dissertation, Dallas Theological Seminary, 1968).

24 See our chapter 4: "The Other Side: Will It Have Any *Redeemable* Occupants?" in our *The Other Side of the Good News*.

25 See our discussion of Luke 16:19-31 in Chapter 5: "The Other Side: According to Jesus" in our *The Other Side of the Good News*.

26 I believe Bell could reword Ferré's statement and say that "Traditional orthodoxy has to be mocked, misstated, and declared toxic."

27 Nels F.S. Ferré, *Evil and the Christian Faith* (New York: Harper & Brothers, 1947), p. 118.

28 Surprisingly, Bell recommends Timothy Keller's study *The Prodigal God* (which emphasizes, I think, the opposite point which Bell is making).

29 See Martin Bashir's interview of Bell where he asks Bell three times: "Is it irrelevant and immaterial about how one responds to Christ in this life in terms of determining one's eternal destiny?" To each instance of the question, Bell responded that belief is vitally important, but never explained why. www.youtube.com/watch?v=Vg-qgmJ7nzA As Bashir said, Bell wants to have it both ways: that salvation is true regardless of one's response and that one's response is absolutely relevant and matters greatly.

30 This sounds very much like the statement by the universalist Philip Gulley who said of Jesus' statement on the cross: "Grace, not justice, was his choice. After his resurrection, having already forgiven his enemies, he saw no need to destroy them." (*If Grace Is True*, p. 80).

31 This reminds one of Berkouwer's challenge to Barth's universalism where Berkouwer writes, "The new situation exists independently of the proclamation or non-proclamation of it. It also exists independently of belief or nonbelief in it. The Kingdom of God 'has its truth in itself, not in that which in pursuance of it happens or does not happen on the earth.'" (*The Other Side of the Good News*, p. 42).

---

[32] John A.T. Robinson, In the End, God (London: James Clarke, 1950), pp. 102-103.

[33] Ferré, The Christian Understanding of God, p. 237.

[34] Hell? Yes!, p. 86.

[35] Those who hold this viewpoint have to purposely overlook Revelation 20:16 which says, "And the devil, who deceived them, was thrown into the lake of burning sulfur, where the beast and the false prophet had been thrown. They will be tormented day and night for ever and ever."

[36] When asked by Bashir why he chose Origen as being part of the orthodox tradition and not Arius (who denied the deity of Jesus), Bell responded by a weak "because I am a pastor."

[37] *If Grace Is True*, p. 18. Universalists often denigrate the authority of the Word of God, as I have shown in Chapter 2 of my *The Other Side of the Good News*, pp. 63ff.

[38] *The Inescapable Love of God*, p. 107. Bell similarly uses I Timothy 1:20 to argue that "the most severe judgment falls squarely within the redemptive purposes of God in the world." (90).

[39] Horton's review is available at: wscal.edu/media/docs/Bells_Hell_Review_by Michael_Horton.pdf.

[40] See Chapter 4 on the issue of after-death opportunities for conversion in my *The Other Side of the Good News*.

[41] Quoted in http://baptistpress.com/BPnews.asp?ID=34843

[42] See Kevin's full review at: http://thegospelcoalition.org/blogs/kevindeyoung/2011/03/14/rob-bell-love-wins-review/

[43] Galli's article on whether Bell is a litmus test for believers makes the point that Bell is a brother through whom the Holy Spirit *might* be raising some significant questions the church ought to be addressing. See our last appendix for a discussion of this perspective.

[44] See his *The Gospel of Inclusion: Reaching Beyond Religious Fundamentalism to the True Love of God* (Azusa Press/ Council Oak Books, 2007) where he says such things as: "Redemption is not a process. Redemption is instantaneous and immediate, the result of the finished work of the Cross. It requires neither action nor belief." (p. 104); "Evangelism is not getting people saved; it is informing people of God's redemptive love towards them. Faith doesn't save you; faith just recognizes that you are saved." (p. 126); "We assume that death is automatic, imposed upon humanity without our consent, but that eternal life comes only by choice and election. God's plan was crafted without our participation or permission, and under His system, all are redeemed, even if the rest of us do not believe they should be. This is amazing grace." (p. 154). In 2010 Pearson also wrote *God Is Not a Christian, Nor a Jew, Muslim, Hindu...: God Dwells with Us, in Us, Around Us, as Us.* So Pearson has not only abandoned the gospel; he has abandoned basic theism.

[45] Quoted in The Other Side of the Good News, p. 119.

[46] Ibid.

[47] Bertrand Russell, Why I Am Not a Christian and Other Essays on Religion and Related Subjects, NY: Simon & Schuster, 1957, p. 17.

[48] Found at http://marshill.org/believe/

[49] Quoted in Jeffress, p. 82.

[50] Larry Dixon, an alumnus of Emmaus Bible College, is the author of *The Other Side of the Good News* (Wheaton, Ill.: BridgePoint, 1992). The book is an examination of contemporary challenges to Jesus' teaching on hell.

[51] Tom Harpur, Life After Death (Willowdale, Ontario: McClelland and Stewart, 1991), 126-127.

[52] Thomas Talbott, "The Doctrine of Everlasting Punishment," Faith and Philosophy 7 (Jan., 1990): 30.

[53] William Crockett, "The Metaphorical View," in Four Views on Hell, ed. William Crockett (Grand Rapids: Zondervan, 1992), 43.

[54] Charles Pickstone, "Fleeing from Infinity: Baudelaire's Vision of Hell," Theology 95 (July/August 1992): 262.

[55] Quoted in Stephen H. Travis, "The Problem of Judgment," Themelios 11 (Jan., 1986): 52.

[56] Clark H. Pinnock, "Response to John F. Walvoord," in Crockett, Four Views on Hell, 39.

[57] Alan W. Gomes, "Evangelicals and the Annihilation of Hell: Part One," Christian Research Journal, (Spring, 1991): 15.

[58] Timothy Phillips, "The Damnation of Hell," (Unpublished paper, Wheaton College Graduate School, March 23, 1991): 4. It seems to me that Kantzer (in his "The Doctrine Wars," Christianity Today, October 5, 1992) misses an opportunity to address this specific issue. That the overhaul of hell signals a departure from other evangelical beliefs is perhaps illustrated by noticing Pinnock's comments about inspiration (e.g., his comment that [the New Testament writers] "surrendered entirely to Hellenism [in their doctrine of man's immortal soul]," Clark H. Pinnock and Delwin Brown, Theological Crossfire (Grand Rapids: Zondervan, 1990), 220, anthropology (e.g., his challenge that "orthodoxy needs to straighten out its anthropology", Four Views on Hell, 149), and the doctrine of God (e.g., his oft-quoted attack: "How can Christians possibly project a deity of such cruelty and vindictiveness whose ways include inflicting everlasting torture upon his creatures, however sinful they may have been? Surely a God who would do such a thing is more nearly like Satan than like God, at least by any ordinary moral standards, and by the Gospel itself," Clark H. Pinnock, "The Destruction of the Finally Impenitent," Criswell Theological Review [Spring, 1990]: 246-247). Pinnock even recommends the doctrine of purgatory ("Belief in purgatory is an ancient tradition just as everlasting conscious punishment is, so I do not see how it can be ruled out of consideration by evangelicals. Perhaps it has even more credibility as a tradition. Ironically, I rather think that it actually does .... Is a doctrine of purgatory not required by our doctrine of holiness?" Four Views on Hell, 129-130).
I agree with Gomes when he says, "The same holy God who 'shall be revealed from heaven with His mighty angels in flaming fire' [2 Thes. 1:7] is the God who stooped to become one of us, and bore the vengeance of God's fire in His own body on the tree. If God should open our eyes to understand the terrible price He paid, we would in that instant comprehend the awful guilt of spurning that price"

("Evangelicals and the Annihilation of Hell: Part Two," Christian Research Journal, [Summer, 1991]: 13).

[59] Henri J. M. Nouwen, *The Way of the Heart* (San Francisco: Harper and Row, 1981), 21.

[60] I am using the term "back-peddling" intentionally. If one is biking down the wrong path, back-peddling might be the wisest action to take. I am contending in this article that the traditional doctrine of hell is, however, the right path.

[61] Clark H. Pinnock, "The Destruction of the Finally Impenitent", CTR, (Spring, 1990): 246-247.

[62] John R. W. Stott and David Edwards, Evangelical Essentials (London: Hodder & Stoughton, 1988), 319-320.

[63] Donald G. Bloesch, Essentials of Evangelical Theology 2 vols. (San Francisco: Harper and Row, 1978), 2:226.

[64] Michael Green, Evangelism Through the Local Church (London: Hodder & Stoughton, 1990), 69.

[65] Ibid., 70. Phillips states that Green's exegetical arguments are unable to handle all the biblical evidence. Green writes: "But what about the lake of fire in the book of Revelation (Rev. 20:10)? That single reference in a highly pictorial book is not enough to hang a doctrine of such savagery on . . . ." (Phillips, "The Damnation of Hell", p. 8).

[66] contra J. I. Packer's description of Bruce's preface as "dissenting" ("Evangelicals and the Way of Salvation," in Evangelical Essentials, eds. Kenneth S. Kantzer and Carl F. H. Henry [Grand Rapids: Zondervan, 1990]), 135.

[67] James Davison Hunter, Evangelicalism: The Coming Generation (Chicago: University of Chicago Press, 1987), 183.

[68] Michael Bauman, Pilgrim Theology: Taking the Path of Theological Discovery (Grand Rapids: Zondervan, 1992), 13. Emphasis mine.

[69] Jonathan Edwards, "Sinners in the Hands of an Angry God," Select Works of Jonathan Edwards, vol. 2, Sermons (London: Banner of Truth Trust, 1959), 183-199.

[70] Ibid.

[71] Ibid.

[72] Ibid. Wouldn't you love to overhear Jonathan Edwards present the gospel to the horror-writer Stephen King?

[73] Clark H. Pinnock, "The Conditional View," in Four Views on Hell, ed. William Crockett, 140.

[74] Ibid., "Response to John F. Walvoord," 38. Pinnock's sarcasm causes him to ridicule Walvoord's defense of the traditional view:
"Has Walvoord visited the burn unit in his local hospital recently? Is he not conscious of the sadism he is attributing to God's actions? I am baffled, knowing that John is a kindly man, how he can accept a view of God that makes him out to be morally worse than Hitler" (Ibid., 38). Pinnock sounds like the second-century critic Celsus who rejected the doctrine of God's judgment with a wave of the hand, arguing that in the traditional view God becomes a "cosmic cook" (Ibid., 50). Pinnock later ridicules "the heroism" of conservatives who hold to the traditional position because they believe the Bible teaches it (Ibid., 143-144).

[75] Ibid., 39.

[76] R. C. Sproul, "The Limits of God's Grace: Jonathan Edwards on Hell," Tabletalk 14 (July, 1990): 4.

[77] Quoted in Haddon Robinson, Biblical Preaching (Grand Rapids: Baker, 1980), 101.

[78] Clark H. Pinnock and Delwin Brown, Theological Crossfire, 226, 227, 230.

[79] Rodney Clapp, "Overdosing on the Apocalypse," Christianity Today (October 28, 1991): 27.

[80] Daniel Fuller, The Unity of the Bible, (pre-publication manuscript., Chapter 13), 239-240.

[81] Ibid., 246.

[82] Timothy R. Phillips, "Hell: A Christological Reflection," in Through No Fault of Their Own? The Fate of Those Who Have Never Heard, eds. William V. Crockett and James G. Sigountos (Grand Rapids: Baker, 1991), 52.

[83] Quoted in John H. Gerstner, Repent or Perish (Ligonier, Pa.: Soli Deo Gloria Pub., 1990), 16.

[84] Nels F. S. Ferré, Christ and the Christian (New York: Harper and Brothers, 1953), 245.

[85] Nels F. S. Ferré, The Christian Understanding of God (London: SCM, 1951), 240.

[86] Millard Erickson, "Is Universalistic Thinking Now Appearing Among Evangelicals?" United Evangelical Action (September/October 1989): 6.

[87] Timothy R. Phillips, Through No Fault of Their Own?, 57. Note also Craig's comment that "the notion that some sinners shall finally repent under the prolonged rigours of purgatory smacks of recantation under torture, and we all know how likely it is that such professions are voluntary or sincere. It seems more likely that sinners under God's punishment will grow even harder in their hearts and more determined in their hatred of Him for treating them thus." (William Lane Craig, "Talbott's Universalism," Religious Studies 27 (1991): 300.

[88] The poena damni is the punishment of the damned, the pain of eternal separation from God. The poena sensus is the punishment of sense, the actual torment suffered by those separated from God for eternity.

[89] William V. Crockett, "Wrath That Endures Forever," Journal of the Evangelical Theological Society 34 (1991):196.

[90] Timothy Phillips, "The Damnation of Hell," 16.

[91] Cited by Harold O. J. Brown in a review of A Wideness in God's Mercy: The Finality of Jesus Christ in a World of Religions, by Clark Pinnock, Christianity Today (September 14, 1992): 40.

[92] Evangelical Essentials, 328. Emphasis mine.

[93] William V. Crockett, "Wrath That Endures Forever," 201.

[94] Larry Dixon, The Other Side of the Good News, Chapter Five, "The Other Side According to Jesus," (Wheaton, Ill.: BridgePoint, 1992).

[95] Timothy R. Phillips, Through No Fault of Their Own? 53. Pinnock states that Jesus did not use speculation about hell in order to press people into a decision for the gospel (Four Views on Hell, 145). I believe Pinnock misreads Jesus here.

See my book The Other Side of the Good News, Chapter Five, "The Other Side According to Jesus."

[96] "Invictus," quoted in Craig, "Talbott's Universalism," 301-302.

[97] John H. Gerstner, *Repent or Perish,* 28.

[98] http://www.christianitytoday.com/ct/article_print.html?id=91797

Made in the USA
Charleston, SC
15 July 2011